DECORATING
WITH Collectibles

Annette R. Lough

Photos without credit lines are courtesy of *Collector's mart* magazine.

© 1997 by Annette R. Lough

Published by

**krause
publications**

700 E. State Street • Iola, WI 54990-0001

Please call or write for our free catalog of publications. Our toll-free number to place an order or to obtain a free catalog is (800) 258-0929. Please use our regular business telephone (715) 445-2214 for editorial comment and further information.

Library of Congress Catalog Number: 96-76693
ISBN: 0-87341-458-6
Printed in the United States of America

With special thanks to . . .

My mother, for her unconditional love and support;

My father, who taught me that doing my best would always pay off;

My much-adored son, who's oftentimes my creative inspiration and always the light of my life;

My husband, whose faith in me makes it possible to go on;

And my sister, who reminds me not to take life too seriously.

My deepest appreciation to the wonderful people in the collectibles industry who've been so kind and generous, and who have offered so much encouragement to this project, particularly Bill and Sandy Bales, who introduced me to the hobby.

Contents

8 Country Charm

The relaxed attitude of life in the country serves up enough charm to seduce even city folk. Our sumptuous showcase of country collectibles—from Amish-inspired art to a bevy of barnyard pals—exudes a simple charm and provides us with an escape from the hustle and bustle of city life.

32 Garden Party

Fresh-cut flowers are a luxury in which we all love to indulge. Their fragrant petals intoxicate us, offering up evocative perfumes. The delicate beauty of their petals seduces us with an unparalleled power. If bright blossoms beckon you, explore a practical alternative: collectibles. A passion for flowers blooms in a bounty of plates, prints, and figurines for all to enjoy.

50 Kids and Collecting

The fun of collecting comes through in a kaleidoscope of collectibles certain to appeal to the young and the young at heart. We'll show you spunky decorating solutions sure to satisfy a sports fan's sweetest dreams, as well as nursery rhyme knickknacks perfect for welcoming a wee one into the wonderful world of collecting.

62 Nautical Nuances

The crashing of waves and the wondrous sight of a seemingly endless sea come to mind when you are a collector of nautical-themed collectibles. Baubles from the beach shine bright when they're actually blown glass ornaments, and beacons of light—many of them lighted stained glass miniatures—beckon "wanna-be" sailors with a welcoming glow.

72 Rustic Retreats

Appointed with casual and comfortable furnishings, you'll think these rustic retreats have been decorated by Mother Nature—with the help of a nature-loving collector, that is. Incorporating a tasteful array of animal life—none of which require feeding—these homes take on the look and feel of a mountain lodge with a covey of collectibles depicting the outdoors.

86 Seasonal Sanctuary

Holidays call for special decor and a delightful display of seasonal collectibles. Easter heralds spring with a vibrant array of bunnies and blossoms. Independence Day sizzles with a sprinkling of stars and stripes. And the celebration of Christmas glistens in the extraordinary gala of gatherings from traditional to contemporary, from the usual to the unique.

120 Southwest Samplings

Explore the spicy spirit of the Southwest—and the art indicative of the region. Pewter pieces recalling the rich history of Native Americans are displayed alongside timeworn antiques, while cavalcades of cowboy kitsch serve up a more relaxed feel and provide plenty of laugh-out-loud humor.

136 Victorian Romance

Charming dolls adorned in linen and lace, plates featuring the angelic children of yesteryear, and miniature cottages recalling the romance of old England—all harken back to a time when elegance was everyday. Come along for a tour of tasteful treasures worked subtly into today's home decor.

Acknowledgments

Photographers: Steve Gerig and Ross Hubbard on behalf of *Collector's mart* magazine, Krause Publications, Iola, Wisconsin.

Photo Styling: Gail Senn Bowen, Jennifer Lee, Annette Lough, Mary Lou Marshall.

Props: Sandy Bales, Gail Senn Bowen, Kathleen Knoll, Mary Sieber.

Special Assistance and Support: Sandy Bales, Connie Boone, Deborah Faupel, Kimberly Graber, Kerrie Green, Mary Lou Marshall, Jan Wojtech, Rossanne Thompson, Mary Sieber.

Thank you to the following businesses: Brown's Botanicals, Wichita, Kansas; The Hourglass, Wichita, Kansas; Master Galleries, Wichita, Kansas; Stanges, Waupaca, Wisconsin.

A special thanks to the homeowners who allowed us to come into their homes, rearrange their lives, and photograph much of the material featured in this book:

Judy Bingman
Joyce Black
Flora Chambers
Judy Douglas
Tom and Stephanie Dye
Danny and Deborah Faupel
Melissa Hamilton
Charlene and Ted Hickok
Mike and Peggy Livingston
Charles and Janet Koehn
Patricia Krause
Jim and Angela McClure
Jeff and Lauren Miller
Helen and Ken Nelson
Debbie and Pat O'Brien
Greg and Sharla Parkhurst
Sheryl and Mark Porter
Deanna Roper and Bob Liebl
Alice Schiefelbein
Sandy and Cecil Ward

Introduction

In recent months, I have come to a conclusion: Nearly everyone collects. Some people don't do it consciously—of course, they are perfectly aware of having an unusual grouping of angels gracing a sunny spot in their kitchen; they realize they have amassed an impressive, if not unique, bounty of teddy bears that are cleverly tucked between antique books in what was once their grandmother's armoire; they may even admit to an avid interest in Southwestern art or Indian artifacts—but they may be completely unaware that by gathering them, they are, in fact, collecting. That's what makes this time-honored tradition so completely wonderful— it's unconscious, free-spirited, and can be carried out on any level. Collectors need not devote their lives, nor their life savings, to acquiring treasures that will bring them joy day in and day out. Collecting is a natural extension of the individuals and the things they love.

A friend of mine has begun countless collections over the past several years. She begins one, tires of that, and adopts another. Kewpie dolls, Cherished Teddies, and Dreamsicles have been the objects of her obsession. I have barely learned of one collection before she has moved on to another.

My mother, on the other hand, has been collecting M. I. Hummel plates and figurines ever since I can remember. They were always a source of awe for my sister and me. Gazing up at those untouchables, we wondered what magic spell they cast over our usually frugal mother. Mom's collection began with the 1970 annual plate, and though she missed a few issues over the years, she has been able to catch up on the series by seeking them out on the secondary market. Along the way, she has begun several other collections, including Longaberger Baskets, Byers' Choice carolers, Hallmark ornaments, animation cels and art prints, and her latest conquest—special issue Barbies.

I, too, am guilty of straying from one collection to another. Precious Moments, Ladie and Friends, Jody Bergsma prints, Walt Disney Classics, Margaret Furlong and Hallmark Keepsake ornaments can be counted among my sometimes short-lived, but much-adored obsessions. But, then, that's the beauty of collecting. There are no rules!

Over the past few years, my involvement with the collectibles industry has included coordinating decorating shoots. The primary purpose of these shoots was to educate collectors on the variety—and increased enjoyment—they could achieve with their collections. No more putting them behind glass where they became "untouchable." Throughout this process, I have gathered dozens of ideas for showcasing my own collections, and the purpose of this book is to share those ideas with you. It is my hope that you will try a few of these simple suggestions and gain more enjoyment from your collection. Good luck and happy collecting!

Country Charm

Most of us would gladly give up city life for a long, romantic weekend in the country: cooking up delights in the kitchen, unwinding on long walks outdoors, and soaking up the solitude of wide open spaces. Country life recalls days when people knew their neighbors. Ice cream socials and county fairs were events in which the whole community pulled together to create the fun.

Today's rural living calls for relaxed attitudes, laid-back furnishings, and casual collectibles. And no matter where you live, you can create that spirit in your own home. All it takes are a few well-chosen pieces indicative of simple country charms.

Limited edition prints of landscapes recapture halcyon days and reflect the nostalgia of yesteryear. A bevy of barnyard critters captures the fun of life on the farm. Dolls, plates, and figurines depicting Amish life serve as reminders that some people still enjoy a slower pace. Kick back, get cozy, and join us for a frolic in the country.

Above: Famous for their trademark eyes (simply two small dots), the Ladie and Friends characters have enjoyed great popularity among collectors. This plucky pair of hare is a heartwarming addition to a country kitchen.

Left: Kitchens are the heart of every home. A tidy and practical addition to any kitchen is a desk that serves as a central location for leaving and retrieving messages or mail. Because this desk also boasts a roomy hutch, it has become the perfect showcase for a kitschy clustering of collectibles. A display of barnyard friends, balanced with a variety of country favorites, combines to create a warm and enjoyable showcase.

Today's rural living calls for relaxed attitudes, laid-back furnishings, and casual collectibles.

Who wouldn't want to wake up to breakfast with a view like this! While the homeowner's spacious windows offer bird-watching at its best, the interior has a pastoral look all its own. The corner provides a cozy niche for countrified collectibles.

Creative Collector Create an intriguing arrangement on your wall by grouping round plates and square prints. Choose items in similar themes and alternate them in a creative pattern. Make sure to leave enough space between each work of art.

An upscale baker's rack lends an interesting focal point and provides a perfect place for collectibles and country crafts—many created by the homeowner. Silk bouquets lend a bright touch of color when placed among the collage of crafts and collectibles.

Once a farmer's castaway chicken coop, this unique unit has become a wonderful place to display treasured items, none more appropriate than the hens and chicks situated among the shelves. The homeowner plays up the depth of the shelves by "layering" items of various heights. Through this technique, not only does she gain additional space, but each item achieves maximum impact. The sides of the unit act as additional space for clustering tiny prints, crafts, and wall hangings.

Left: Take full advantage of your armoire as did this collector. She has thrown open the doors of the cupboard and filled it with items she's spent years gathering. By staggering items at various heights and depths upon the shelves, she has added interest to her display. Dried flowers, heirloom linens, and handwoven baskets add texture and create contrast. Using tiny nails, she has even attached hanging items inside the doors. Don't overlook the space on top, which can become an attractive focal point in itself.

You don't have to cram collectibles into a single space. Spread them out for maximum viewing. For a nostalgic country look, mix plates and miniature facades with wooden animals atop oak furniture. The key to creating a cohesive look is to keep items within the same theme. Here, Amish-inspired art creates an air of simplicity.

Think you've run out of room? Don't overlook display space. This oak end table accommodates items even on the lower shelf.

Above: These swags are created simply with fresh greenery and a sampling of sea stars. (Margaret Furlong Designs, Salem, Ore.)

Right: An oak armoire harbors a dynamic grouping of porcelain ornaments. Threaded on transparent fishing line and hung along the interior, they provide an elegant backdrop. Boughs of fresh greenery add some spirited pizzazz. Faux evergreens stand sentry, anchoring the look. (Margaret Furlong Designs, Salem, Ore.)

Above: Amish-inspired items exude a simple charm when displayed against the rich cherry of this handsome secretary. Plates featuring the art of P. Buckley Moss strike a chord of simpler times—something we all long for occasionally.

Left: Miniature architectural facades create a cheery community atop this sunny windowsill. The collector has carefully selected pieces that complement her home furnishings. (FJ Designs, Wooster, Ohio)

The addition of this Shaker shelf greatly increased the amount of display area for this collector. Amish-themed plates and platters are intermixed with architectural miniatures to create a lively display serenading the simple life. (Brick Works, Cedar Rapids, Iowa)

Heirloom treasures and painted accessories accompany these creative architectural elements to create a cozy corner in this guest room. Actually hand-painted bricks, these facades have become highly collectible. (Brick Works, Cedar Rapids, Iowa)

Creative Collector Line wooden building facades (Shelia's and Cat's Meow are two popular collectible lines) atop doors, cabinets, and even picture frames. To keep them from toppling, place a little "earthquake" putty or museum wax on their bottoms or backsides.

Above: The doors were removed from the lower cabinets on this dry sink, making an accessible and attractive place for display. Dolls in a variety of themes are grouped in an intriguing arrangement. (The Ashton-Drake Galleries, Niles, Ill.)

Left: The Amish influence has certainly made its presence known in the collectibles field. Here, tiny vignettes featuring a variety of Ashton-Drake designs are spread throughout the room, lending a cozy feel. The look is supported by authentic Amish quilts crafted in cheery calico fabrics. (The Ashton-Drake Galleries, Niles, Ill.)

Who wouldn't be ready to snuggle up with a good book and unwind in this inviting reading area? Whimsical plates depicting the lighthearted humor of artist Charles Wysocki are mixed with Amish-themed dolls to reflect a rural style that is thoroughly country. (The Ashton-Drake Galleries, Niles, Ill.)

Collectibles are much more special when they reflect our own interests and personalities.

Above: Don't overlook the frequently unused space above cabinets. Why? It makes a terrific place for elegant untouchables. Here, a grouping of Charles Wysocki plates is tucked between work and storage areas. The display makes an effective use of space while sprucing up an otherwise ordinary area. (The Bradford Exchange, Niles, Ill.)

Left: Perhaps you've overlooked your kitchen as a place to display your cherished treasures. This homeowner makes effective use of space high above the hustle and bustle of her work area to create a look that is completely livable. In this particular situation, the oak molding is finished with a deep groove that serves as a plate rail. To mimic the look, hang plates high on the wall. Use wire plate hangers for unframed plates. (The Bradford Exchange, Niles, Ill.)

Plates hung in a vertical display create a much-needed focal point and help break up large wall space. The display is complemented by an effective arrangement along the plate rail and is anchored by the plates harbored in the hutch. (The Bradford Exchange, Niles, Ill.)

Farmyard friends and country collectibles are gathered inside this cheery hutch. The stark white backdrop is a bold contrast against the colorful array of accompaniments.

Above: The unique painting treatment performed on this hutch complements the treasures tucked inside. Teapots, pitchers, and dinnerware can be easily rearranged for a new look or changed seasonally. For added interest, line the back of shelves with large platters, tall plates, or cheery fabric. Smaller items fill in bare spots. (Enesco Corp., Itasca, Ill.)

Right: A handcrafted wagon, brightly painted, cradles a spirited collection of Attic Babies and offers a touch of whimsy. An old wagon, wheelbarrow, or baby buggy could be used in a similar fashion.

Garden Party

*I*f you're a horticulturist at heart, the long winter months can seem unbearable. The rich hues of fall fade slowly as Mother Nature dons her winter coat. Once sunny skies fill with gray clouds, and the sun may not shine for days.

The good news is that the interior of your home doesn't have to be as bleak as the forecast. Splash some spring-like color on your walls, force a gay grouping of bulbs to bloom indoors, and gather a collection of treasures that echo the playful palette of spring.

A few carefully chosen collectibles proclaiming your love of spring can warm your home year round. Peony covered plates, porcelain pansies, and prints depicting Mother Nature's finest flowers are certain to turn your home into a garden oasis.

A few carefully chosen collectibles proclaiming your love of spring can warm your home year round.

Left: The delicate flowers in this room create an extravagant impression. Honeyed walls play home to Lena Liu's floral fantasy, while blooms abound from every direction. The same colors and patterns are repeated in Fenton art glass and accessories for a cohesive and consistent look.

Right: If your love of gardening equals your appreciation for fine art, then the serene elegance of Lladró is certain to tickle your fancy. The fame of the world-renowned figurines, created by the legendary Lladró family, is the equivalent of the tradition of English rose gardens. This pair appears to be gathering a bounty of blooms—likely a bouquet for mother. Perhaps they remind the collector of her own children. (Lladró USA, Moonachie, N.J.)

Create comfortable living spaces in rooms you once ignored.

This flower-strewn bath takes on the air of outdoors and provides the perfect place for pampering. The cozy charm is accomplished by incorporating a variety of collectibles that celebrate the vivid variations of Mother Nature's palette.

Above: Create comfortable living spaces in rooms you once ignored. This mud room, perfectly suited for housing the home-owner's makeshift potting bench, boasts a botanical bounty year round. Summer's harvest is air-dried for fall enjoyment. A vibrant print, reflective of the room's surroundings and the occupant's love of gardening, provides the perfect finishing touch.

Above: An innocent trio of cherubs adds a carefree touch to fresh greenery. Simply suspend them from fishing line or ribbon for an angelic appeal. (Hallmark Cards, Kansas City, Mo.)

Right: Hallmark miniatures add a touch of whimsy to these festive votive candles. You can duplicate the project with your own holiday favorites. Use a hot glue gun to attach greenery and garland to tiny terra cotta flower pots. Tie on ornaments with tiny ribbon or attach them with floral wire. (Hallmark Cards, Kansas City, Mo.)

Forget paper plates and party favors—a bridal shower is cause for a swanky celebration. These bisque angels, set against a back-drop of fresh-cut flowers, sing praise to the vows of everlasting love. Use them to decorate the bride's cake or as placeholders. Present the bride-to-be with her own "starter" collection—a gift she is sure to cherish forever. (Margaret Furlong Designs, Salem, Ore.)

If florals tickle your fancy, you'll want to achieve maximum impact. Repeat the botanical bounty depicted in your collection with wreath and floral designs of the same variety. If roses are the theme in your collectibles, display a dried bouquet or a silk arrangement nearby. If you prefer not to make them yourself, take two or three of your favorite collectibles to a florist and have her or him create something to complement their character.

This beautifully set service harkens back to times when "taking tea" was an everyday, though elegant, ritual. Margaret's Furlong's "Stars by the Yard" encircle the exquisite silver tea set, an heirloom certain to be handed down from one generation to the next. (Margaret Furlong Designs, Salem, Ore.)

Left: "Stars by the Yard," interwoven with colorful greenery, festoon the front of this open-door hutch, while tiny treasures are tucked carefully inside. Each of Margaret Furlong's ornaments comes with a Lucite stand so they can be enjoyed year round without needing to be hung. Their sleek simplicity makes them all the more alluring, especially when contrasted against boughs of boxwood. (Margaret Furlong Designs, Salem, Ore.)

Below: A winding vine of star garlands intertwined with ivy weaves its magic upon a variety of surfaces, providing a simple touch of elegance. The endless array of decorating possibilities provides the catalyst for this highly creative collector. (Margaret Furlong Designs, Salem, Ore.)

Right: Artist Glynda Turley's romantic florals are available on everything from note cards to scented soap. Here a tasseled box serves a practical purpose in the guest bath. The walls are decked in a paper border of like design. The homeowner has completed the look with a limited edition print boasting the richly hued roses and pale pansies that have made Turley a favorite among collectors. (The Art of Glynda Turley, Heber Springs, Ark.)

Below: The romantic art of Glynda Turley, once strictly limited to her paintings, has made its way into the world of gift and home decor. The floral motif featured in the limited edition print is mimicked by the wallpaper border and tapestry pillow. (The Art of Glynda Turley, Heber Springs, Ark.)

Sleep easy and let gentle dreams kiss you goodnight. This elegantly appointed guest room combines prints and plaids—an increasingly popular trend in home decorating. The patterns don't overpower and actually complement one another. Glynda Turley's romantic art, echoed in a variety of items, is the homeowner's cohesive theme. (The Art of Glynda Turley, Heber Springs, Ark.)

You'll find ornaments in a variety of themes from traditional to contemporary. Artist Christopher Radko is renowned for his unique variations of both. Dried hydrangeas and silk flowers embellish the boughs of this elegant wreath. An unusual bunch of berries—actually highly collectible blown glass ornaments—provides an elegant and everlasting touch of color. Come Christmas, these ornaments will look just as lovely upon your Yuletide tree. (Christopher Radko Designs, Dobbs Ferry, N.Y.)

Right: Crossover collecting continues to inspire artists and collectors alike. By mixing media, you increase your overall enjoyment and your ability to create intriguing arrangements. Here, plates surround a single print that provides the key focal point. (The Bradford Exchange, Niles, Ill.)

Left: A bold use of color covers the windows and complements the vertical placement of this collage of collector plates. Their floral theme is echoed in the flower arrangement situated center stage. (The Bradford Exchange, Niles, Ill.)

The playful magic of friends and fairies has become a popular theme among artists as they strive to reconnect us with our inner child.

"Step right up and make yourself at home."

Left: "Step right up and make yourself at home" signals this cozy country sun porch. Boasting an amusing group of barnyard pals, the stoop offers a relaxing area upon which to unwind. Beware of placing items in direct sunlight or where they will be danger of sustaining damage from inclement weather.

Left: Many collectible lines, such as the Krystonia characters pictured here, have story lines that put each piece into their own unique place within the collection. Books, fully illustrated with depictions of the figurines, detail imaginary family histories, conflicts between the characters, and elaborate settings. They provide a great way to share reading material and collectibles with children who delight in the way the characters come to life upon the written page.

Right: Frank Baum's epic tale The Wizard of Oz has become one of the most famous films of all time. Collectibles depicting the story's characters have enjoyed increasing popularity over the years. With a click of your heels and a little know-how, you can easily fabricate this fantasy wreath. Begin by covering a foam ring with shocks of dried wheat that can be easily pushed into the form. Attach silk sunflowers (dried ones look great too) and weave wire-edged ribbon about. Affix ornaments with hot glue or insert them with U-shaped floral pins. (Hallmark Cards, Kansas City, Mo.)

A growing
trend toward
everything
outdoors has
made its
way into
collectibles.

Previous page: Angelic adornments, sleekly sculpted in a solitary shade of white bisque, juxtapose nicely against a backdrop of colorful porcelain. The carefree arrangement combines pieces scoured from flea markets while incorporating cherished heirlooms handed down for generations. The result is a pleasing orchestration of old and new. (Margaret Furlong Designs, Salem, Ore.)

Left: The timeless tradition of tea is one that requires understated elegance. Wound with lively flowering honeysuckle vines, a lovely silver candelabra comes to life—a daring use of everyday items. A single angel ornament, easily fastened to the stems with florist's wire, presides over the sophisticated table setting. (Margaret Furlong Designs, Salem, Ore.)

Below: Surrounded by quaint keepsakes and specimens of the sea, this potted topiary allows us to feel a part of the outdoors year round. The porcelain sea stars are actually ornaments—case in point that they can be used as decorative accessories year round. (Margaret Furlong Designs, Salem, Ore.)

Left: Your favorite gardener is sure to dig this irresistible gift basket. Department 56's *Village Greenhouse*, a gardening element certain to be enjoyed year round, is surrounded by botanical goodies. Everything will be put to practical use, including the basket, which will hold the fruits of the grower's labor. (Department 56, Eden Prairie, Minn.)

Right: The intricate detail achieved with the bas-relief method of casting conveys a realistic three-dimensional appearance. This collector welcomes spring with an innovative and original decorating idea that incorporates ornaments. You can re-create this bird and butterfly wreath in a matter of minutes. With floral wire, secure eucalyptus branches to a grapevine wreath. Glue on dried hydrangeas, moss, and a prefabricated bird's nest (all available at your local craft store). Add an appropriate array of ornaments. (Hallmark Cards, Kansas City, Mo.)

A growing trend toward everything outdoors has made its way into collectibles. Here, the industry's most famous characters— the Precious Moments gang—provide a delightfully decorative touch to an otherwise "dirty" deed. The earthenware is crafted to withstand the elements of the outdoors, and offers an extension of the indoor collection. (Enesco Corp., Itasca, Ill.)

"When I was a kid..."

Kids and Collecting

Collectors are kids at heart. They love the thrill of the hunt, the chance to boast their latest find, and the opportunity to play in the land of make-believe that collecting creates.

Kids—yes, the younger set—revel in the excitement of collecting as well. Fun-loving figurines, dreamy dolls, and treasures they'll cherish for years provide the impetus for saving allowances and extending care to their hard-earned procurements. Let your kids cultivate their architectural tendencies with villages and the accessories that make them come to life. Encourage children to collect their favorite animation characters or super heroes depicted on an abundance of ornaments, plates, and prints. Even Barbie has made her way into the collectibles realm in special issue dolls, ornaments and figurines.

So put on your thinking cap, and cuddle up with your kids for a look into the little one's magical world of collecting.

Trying to score a home run with your child? The all-American theme of baseball is played out nicely in this young boy's bedroom. Bats and balls from dad's days on the mound add a nostalgic touch and provide for hours of "when I was a kid" stories to be shared.

Left: What better decorating theme for a kid's room than that of the world's most famous mouse? Mickey's high-flying Disney pal, Peter Pan, makes an appearance alongside Goofy, Donald, and Captain Hook. As the children grow up, these eternal favorites can be passed on to another generation, providing years of enjoyment.

Right: Sports, of course, is a popular theme among young children. Capitalize on an activity or theme that already interests your child and let him or her try collecting. Here, fine—but fun and affordable—collectibles are surrounded by sports regalia to achieve attractive and entertaining surroundings for your little all-star.

These adorable Ladie and Friends characters definitely capture the spirit of childhood! And they're certain to capture the heart of a young collector! The Sandicast canine (created by artist Sandra Brue) offers a realistic alternative to the real thing, and you can bet you won't have to walk him.

How about an innovative way to present your child with a gift? For each birthday choose a new piece from his or her favorite collectible line and use it as a cake topper. Many pieces even signify their numerical birthday, such as one year old, five years old, and so on. Precious Moments and Little Emmett are two such appropriate collectible lines.

Left: Combining kid's favorites—the zoo, circus animals, and man's best friend—a brightly painted wall shelf adds pizzazz to this little collector's room. The bookends provide a practical contribution while helping to carry out the theme.

Below: It may not be the "Big Top," but one can't help but crack a smile at this charming cavalcade of clowns. The art of Emmett Kelly, Jr. offers an amusing arrangement, while a cheery clown by Karen Germany cajoles a chuckle or two atop this occasional table. Add a special touch by borrowing toys from the kids (let them pick a few favorites) to lay alongside. Children will thrill at the chance to become involved and are sure to produce some creative ideas of their own. Let them create a similar display in their room—a surefire way to get them to clean up, if only temporarily.

Left: Personalized collectibles are all the rage! Use this inscribed ornament instead of a place card at your next dinner party. Or print invitations on an ornament and send it through the mail. Who could resist responding to such an innovative invitation? (Hallmark Cards, Kansas City, Mo.)

Below: Your young Barbie lover will delight in her very own wreath. Help her create it or whip it up yourself as a sentimental surprise. (Hallmark Cards, Kansas City, Mo.)

Creative Collector Looking for a unique idea to present to your favorite mother-to-be? Fill a basket, diaper bag, or pail with cloth diapers, bottles, and other baby essentials. Personalize your gift with an appropriate collectible or an ornament to welcome the newborn into the world. Your gift could be the catalyst for a new collection.

Collecting teaches children responsibility and helps them develop an appreciation for fine things.

With a wonderful array of collectibles conveying children's themes, the nursery makes a perfect haven for sleeping babes. Mother Goose classics have made their way from the pages of rhyme books to the field of collectibles. The folk-art feel of these resin figures gives them an heirloom quality. (Midwest of Cannon Falls, Cannon Falls, Minn.)

Perfectly suited to partying, these Pocket Dragons conjure up images of mischief. Their magical world of make-believe is enough to make us believe they really do exist. As baking brings out the best in these playful creatures, the kitchen appears an appropriate place for them to call home.

Letting children have a say in home decor—holiday or everyday—makes them feel important.

Kids and collecting go hand in hand. After all, we usually discover our collecting instincts at a young age. Perhaps you remember your first collection, whether it be stamps, Barbies, bottle caps, or trains. Or maybe you've gotten your own child involved with the hobby.

Collecting teaches children responsibility and helps them develop an appreciation for fine things. An eager young collector is more likely to save hard-earned cash for that next issue in a series than to fritter it away on candy and junk toys. One thing that intrigues my little guy is the possibility that his collectibles may someday increase in value.

If you consider starting a collection for your youngster, make sure to choose something in which he or she has a genuine interest. Don't assume you know what your child likes. Let your child choose an appealing collectible category. Items procured for your child, which may actually only interest you, will soon be neglected or altogether forgotten. Select the first few pieces of a collection together. After that, you'll have an idea where your child's interests lie and you'll feel confident enough to choose new pieces as gifts.

Above: When you nestle Christmas collectibles with favorite toys old and new, you have a heart-warming and highly sentimental seasonal display. Let your child choose the toys and help plan the "town." You'll be surprised at the innovative ideas your children contribute and the joy they derive from helping. (Department 56, Eden Prairie, Minn.)

Left: Imagine your child's delight when he or she gets a peek at this delightful menagerie. Jewel-tone baubles add a festive flair to this miniature tree, providing just the right spark for igniting holiday magic. (Midwest of Cannon Falls, Cannon Falls, Minn.)

Collectors are kids at heart.

Give grandma a special plate of cookies baked by her favorite grandchildren. Attach an ornament (no fat, zero calories) for her to keep long after the baked goods have been reduced to crumbs. (Hallmark Cards, Kansas City, Mo.)

Create a treasure-laced treat in the kitchen. This tasty vignette, surrounded by seasonal sweets, puts a new spin on the old gingerbread house. Let the kids make winding walking paths lined with gumdrops, or create snow-covered bushes using marshmallows. A sprinkling of powdered sugar will give your scene the look of new-fallen snow. (Department 56, Eden Prairie, Minn.)

Every little girl enjoys taking tea. Here, our old pal Ann is gussied up with a playful porcelain heart pennant—actually a Margaret Furlong ornament. Presents shine even brighter when festive keepsakes serve as bows. (Margaret Furlong Designs, Salem, Ore.)

If you consider starting a collection for your child, make sure to choose something in which he or she has a genuine interest.

Everybody is happy when children have something to call their own. What little lad or lass wouldn't love to help dress up this window seat? Letting children have a say in home decor—holiday or everyday—makes them feel important and provides for special memories that they will pass along to their children. (Department 56, Eden Prairie, Minn.)

Left: Don't limit fun themes to children's rooms. Bring a little fun and festivity to the rest of the house. Your kids will delight in decorative surprises you designed with them in mind.

Creative Collector

When placing collectibles in a child's room, try reusable putty or museum wax to adhere them to shelves or display surfaces. That way, if the surface is accidentally bumped, chances are the precious pieces won't tumble to the ground.

What little skater wouldn't be warmed by this winter scene? Stationed in the mud room, this rustic table, graced with a serendipitous skating scene, conjures up memories of frigid fun on the ice. (Department 56, Eden Prairie, Minn.)

Nautical Nuances

I consider myself a water person. I dream of leisurely afternoons spent walking on white sand. I long to comb the beach, taking home treasures washed in by the tide. I revel in listening to the shrill cries of seagulls soaring overhead.

Unfortunately, my "beach" house sits smack in the middle of America, far from any ocean, miles from any sea. But that's just a technicality, for among my collectibles—bisque sea stars, miniature sea urchins, and blown glass conch shells—nautical shapes give way to imaginary seascapes.

There is a whole trunkful of oceanic treasures awaiting collectors. Miniature lighthouses mimic the majestic sentries towering over restless seas, and place siren calls that lure collectors to procure them. Aqueous wildlife sculptures— dolphin, sea lion, and shark—depict the graceful moves of water creatures, romancing collectors with their sleek shapes. With the right decorating touches applied to collectibles inspired by the sea, you too can imagine sandy shores and sunshine surrounding your home, wherever it may lie.

Left: The owners of this contemporary haven quietly situated on the Kansas plains have vowed to let Heaven and Nature sing! Traditional angels trumpet songs of joy while an arresting array of tropical treasures laud the praises of the sea. The tree is draped in a sparkly sampling of starfish, mermaids, and conch shells—a far cry from traditional decorating fare.

Treasure the grace and beauty of marine life, even if you are miles from any ocean!

Artist Margaret Furlong's signature sea shells lend a tropical touch to this otherwise ordinary topiary, which creates a unique centerpiece. A colorful school of saltwater fish encircle a sentimental selection of Santas—a theme most collectors have found can be displayed year round.

Fill a large clear glass vase or bowl with blown glass ornaments. Mix in natural elements such as pine cones, sea shells, or polished rocks. Use as a centerpiece or tuck into a bookcase to add a spot of color.

Left: A few shells add interest to this seafaring selection of nautical treasures. Natural light, streaming through a wall of full-length windows, casts a luminous glow upon this nautical collection. By grouping miniature ships, lighthouses, and water-themed wildlife, the display becomes more prominent and takes on the feel of a "setting." Line the backs of shelves with starfish or postcards featuring famous ports of call.

Right: Entertaining takes a new light with a playful array of glass bottles, sherbet-colored dinnerware, and lively linens. Effervescent blown glass baubles dangle overhead, adding interest to the light fixture. Porcelain ornaments welcome diners to their place setting and double as party favors.

Left: This bright buoy, anchored with fresh evergreen and baubles borrowed from the beach, makes an arresting backdrop. The featured beacon of light takes center stage, reflecting the sights and sounds of the sea. The display, situated in the entry, serves as a warm welcome to weary sailors. (Department 56, Eden Prairie, Minn.)

What could be more appropriate than a nautical-themed display situated tubside? A miniature tree, sparkling with boats, buoys, and barnacle baubles, adds a playful touch to quiet quarters. Showcase year round for an elegant look in your guest bath. Change your ornaments to reflect different themes, holidays, or seasons.

There is a whole trunkful of oceanic treasures awaiting collectors.

Create a tubside retreat by placing a collection of miniature lighthouses in your private bath. The display will take you to another time and place as you enjoy a relaxing soak. Shredded stuffing—usually used for gift wrap—gives the illusion of water.

Left: An antiquing find indeed, this distinctive dinghy makes an amusing arbor for a grouping of these salient "sentries of the seas." Shells—collectibles created by Mother Nature—fill a tiny tin-punched keepsake box, providing just a taste of the beauty the majestic waters hold in store. A wooden sailboat and salty sailor add a touch of humor. (Harbour Lights, La Mesa, Calif.)

Creative Collector

To eliminate sliding, secure plates or figurines onto furniture or shelves using putty or museum wax, available at hobby and craft stores. Just a dab on the bottom and your collectible will stick to the surface. Neither product is harmful to furniture finishes or art surfaces, and the putty can be reused again and again. It is especially useful in regions where earthquakes are common.

The rich history of the sailor's landmark offers an enduring subject to those with a love for the sea, creating a niche for enthusiasts of lighthouse collectibles. Nautical touches such as conch shells and sea biscuits give this mantle a natural element. The lighted replicas capture the lure of these historical icons. (Forma Vitrum, Cornelius, N.C.)

Dream of leisurely afternoons spent walking on white sand. Revel in listening to the shrill cries of seagulls soaring overhead.

Above: Looks like somebody is dining at the captain's table this evening! Imagine the dinner conversation when you create an allur-ing arrangement such as this. Featuring an arresting array of lighthouses and accessories influenced by the sea, this celebration of sentinels makes a delightful addition to any meal. (Harbour Lights, La Mesa, Calif.)

Left: This masculine arrangement takes on the sights and sounds of the sea with elegant Lladró figures. The luminous hues are trademark of the fine Italian porcelain makers whose pieces are highly sought after on the primary *and* secondary markets. (Lladró USA, Moonachie, N.J.)

Rustic Retreats

Who can walk by a bookcase without investigating what musings await exploration?

*E*ach and every day we're faced with the hustle and bustle of life—careers, kids, concerns over bills, daily details. These are the things that control our "free" time, until there is no "freedom" left to enjoy.

Because responsibilities rule our lives, rarely are we able to find time to curl up with a good book, or spare even a few hours for hiking, biking, hunting, or fishing. But a home inspired by the freedom of the great outdoors allows us to enjoy some of those pursuits without ever leaving the house.

Back to the basics doesn't mean roughing it. Far from it. The lodge look, one of today's most recognized styles, has conveyed the call of the wild to many homeowners. The style incorporates natural elements in a relaxed atmosphere—paring down for less clutter and bringing nature indoors. Here, feathered fowl take flight among prints depicting lush fields of flora and fauna. Fish swim their way into serene settings as figurines, woodcarvings, or ornaments. Gamesmen hunt their prey as sculpture, nutcrackers, or tree trimmings, reflecting the outdoorsmen's favorite pursuits.

The warmth of these rustic retreats welcomes one into an existence of solitude, perfectly suited to a quiet evening around the fire. So pull up an overstuffed chair, sit back, and take refuge in a covey of collectibles designed with nature in mind.

Right: Who can walk by a bookcase without investigating what musings await exploration? Their sturdy shelves provide perfect niches for displaying treasures gathered over time. To create depth and inject interest into the display area, integrate items in a variety of shapes, sizes, and textures. Line shelves with rich tapestries that mimic the room's powerful color scheme. Use plate hangers or cup hooks to make the most of shelf space and increase your exhibit area.

Left: Who wouldn't relish a few hours tucked away in the quiet solitude of this den? The rich hues of the tapestries imitate the crisp feel of autumn and inject a bit of warmth into an otherwise roughcast room. Wall-mounted trophies and well-positioned treasures speak volumes about the outdoor interests enjoyed by the nature-loving homeowners.

Left: Decoys sporting vivid hues of plumage mirror the room's rustic feel and are effortlessly nestled into the surroundings.

Back to the basics
doesn't mean
roughing it.

Above: Par for the course, this delightful display of sports collectibles is certain to score points with a golfer. Collectibles reflecting the interests of a loved one make great gifts and will be cherished for years to come.

Below left: This richly appointed entry greets guests with a hearty declaration of outdoorsmanship. Steins adorned with exquisitely detailed pewter lids exert a masculine feel. A lidded stein is a tradition that dates back to the days when German children were sent to taverns to fetch the day's ale. A eucalyptus swag, bearing bunches of dried pods and berries, provides texture and softens the scene more so than a print.

Below: By appointing our homes with what we know and love best, we provide ourselves a private sanctuary in which to revel. Mementos of past fishing trips and family vacations are carefully grouped to serve as a simple reminder of life's precious moments.

Creative Collector

In regions where earthquakes are common, use some preventative measures for protecting collectibles. To keep them from toppling, string taut fishing line across the front of shelves and bookcases. Research the cost of earthquake insurance, which may be less expensive than you'd think.

Left: Use everyday items to help illustrate your collection. Hand-carved fishing lures festoon this antique chest, adding interest to an otherwise bare corner. The right touches—fishing creel, bamboo poles, hand-painted pike, and a realistic mixed media sculpture—convey a strong sense of time and place.

Right: The rugged feel of this rustic home is softened by southern sunlight streaming through full-length glass. By mixing architectural styles, the home becomes more personable. The hand-hewn wood railing, crafted by the homeowners themselves, is a nice contrast to the elegant arches framing the windows. A Sandicast sculpture, looking like the real thing, is positioned so it can take full advantage of the sun. Other elements, artfully arranged, impart a love of the outdoors.

Right: Year round, the quiet corner of this reading room provides the homeowners with a window to the outdoors. Schools of artificial fish are held swimmingly by equally artificial tree branches, luring one to discover what other mysteries might await.

The warmth of these rustic retreats
welcomes one into an existence of solitude.

The vast offerings in wildlife art provide plenty of impetus for getting your favorite sportsman to collect.

Inexpensive items gleaned from tag sales often create the most impact. Here, a colorful and eclectic array of Fiestaware takes center stage in an old armoire. A row of ducks provides a pleasing frame for the plaid matted print. A fishing vignette (in which the Gus doll from Wild Wings is the key element) lures one to explore a unique arrangement of angler's accouterments.

Left: Don't limit your enjoyment of collectibles to the living room! As a professional pastry chef and highly sought-after "chocolatier," this homeowner spends a lot of time whipping up tasty treats in the kitchen. This cozy nook harbors musings and mementos that she can enjoy while she works.

Santas have become a popular year-round collectible. This rough-cast dual mantle provides the perfect place to display a vast collection of Briercroft creations. (Briercroft, Winchester, Ind.)

Creative Collector Tie tiny fish ornaments onto brass or wood candleholders using twine or natural raffia.

A cozy haven in which to retreat after a long day, this bedroom imparts the style of a seasoned collector. Plates fastened into wood frames (available in most gift stores and galleries) line the walls with scenes of feathered friends. Forget the rule of only positioning items at eye level. The bold placement of these plates not only makes a statement, it creates interest at otherwise plain points on the walls. Go as high as you wish, but be beware of hanging anything lower than four feet, especially if little ones still live at home. (The Bradford Exchange, Niles, Ill.)

Above: This serene setting provides a place for quiet respite while incorporating a hunter's favorite sights—those depicting the sporting life. The vast offerings in wildlife art provide plenty of impetus for getting your favorite sportsman to collect. Terry Redlin, perhaps the most popular artist in this particular genre, creates rustic settings that convey the "intricate simplicity" of nature.

Below: This sportsman has pulled a trunkful of treasures out and placed them on top for all to see. The stunning display, incorporating an eclectic array of wildlife, serves as a reminder that hunting season is not far away.

Seasonal Sanctuary

*H*olidays spent with family and friends are some of the happiest times in our lives. Surrounded by loved ones, celebrating the joy of the season—whichever one that may be—provides us with memories that will be forever treasured.

Treasured collectibles indicative of the appropriate holiday are happy additions to any seasonal celebration. By decking your halls with the opulent elegance of Christmas, the phrase "season's greetings" takes on a whole new meaning. Snow villages, ornaments, and nutcrackers add a special spark to the Yuletide festivities.

Easter ornaments, prints, plates, and figurines depicting cheery chicks and bunnies herald the start of spring, bringing with them hope that April showers will eventually give way to May flowers. Halloween, Thanksgiving, and Independence Day all have their own unique introductions and issues, certain to delight the seasonal collector.

These celebratory items not only bring joy to a single generation, but are certain to become heirlooms passed on to children and grandchildren. Get ready for a decoupage of seasonally inspired decorating ideas destined to delight the creative collector in you.

Treasured collectibles indicative of the appropriate holiday are happy additions to any seasonal celebration.

All aglow and set to incite Christmas cheer, this breathtaking home sparkles with seasonal style. Every nook and cranny beholds an arresting collection bound to intrigue. Not enough branches on the tree to hold all of the ornaments you've amassed over the years? The garland, wrapped along the arch and spindles, features a fetching array of blown glass baubles from Old World Christmas, Midwest of Cannon Falls, and Kurt S. Adler. Use wire hooks or florist's wire to hang ornaments from the boughs. For more impact, tie them on with tiny ribbons, gold cord or raffia. Add silk poinsettias or sprigs of holly.

Spruce up a traditional holiday wreath by incorporating a few unique ingredients. Using boxwood as opposed to ordinary evergreen, this design featuring a Department 56 miniature puts your cherished cottage center stage. Mount your piece into place using spray foam or a hot glue gun and floral picks. By carefully disguising the cord, you can still light up your scene. A small strand of battery operated lights would certainly do the trick. (Department 56, Eden Prairie, Minn.)

Right: Don't be afraid to tie one on—to your tree skirt, that is! A seasonal sampling of merry miniatures can certainly add a touch of whimsy beneath the tree. Simply sew on the tiny treasures using decorative ribbon or embroidery thread. (Hallmark Cards, Kansas City, Mo.)

A lavish table setting gains added sophistication when accompanied by an extravagant centerpiece and tapered candles. The jewel-like glow of Christopher Radko's blown glass ornaments adds the crowning touch to this unique topiary, which is artfully surrounded by an equally innovative bounty of sparkling treasures. (Christopher Radko, Dobbs Ferry, N.Y.)

DECORATING WITH THE PROS

Instead of devoting an entire room to your collection, Tom Underwood, a stylist for Department 56—famous makers of villages and accessories—suggests laying out small vignettes throughout your home, incorporating just two or three collectible pieces into each display.

"Pick a theme and then carry it throughout the house," says Tom. "Create scenes that are related to individual rooms such as the office or den."

Some of Tom's favorite props include terra cotta pots, flat slate stone, baskets, and old wooden planter boxes. He suggests taking cues from your home decor and playing up what you already have. "It doesn't have to be expensive," says Tom. "This is something you can have fun with."

Tom also suggests letting little ones help. He says he re-creates memories from his own childhood when setting up scenes. "It's great anytime kids can express themselves," says Tom. "Kids love it. Let them create displays in their bedroom—perhaps on the headboard of their bed. Or use the village pieces as night-lights. When those kids are older, they're going to be fighting over the highly collectible and much-loved houses."

Decking the halls—as the collector has done upon this marble-topped hall table—takes on a new tone when the featured items form such a unique arrangement. Brilliant color and candle-light emanate from this magical array of orna-ments. Bright pink and shades of silver and blue vary from the usual hues most commonly asso-ciated with Christmas. (Christopher Radko Designs, Dobbs Ferry, N.Y.)

Display your affection for collectibles year round, but don't forget to capitalize on the holidays.

Creative Collector

A simple branch painted white or left natural perfectly displays a collection of spring or Easter-themed orna-ments. Insert the main branch into a cube of floral foam. Secure the branch with hot glue. "Plant" the stem in a ceramic pot or basket, deep enough to hold the foam and stabilize the weight of the "tree." Cover the foam with Spanish moss or colored Easter grass. Tie orna-ments to twigs with pastel ribbon or natural raffia. Nest clusters of tiny eggs around the base.

Creative Collector Don't be afraid to display your Christmas tree year round. While miniature trees are less intrusive, a full-size faux fir or spruce can serve as an effective and impressive display. Decorate it with ornaments and keepsakes celebrating themes such as Valentine's Day, Easter, or Thanksgiving. Or takes cues from your home decor such as country, Victorian, or Southwestern. One collector showcases a grand display of Independence Day memorabilia year round.

Above: Display your affection for collectibles year round, but don't forget to capitalize on the holidays. Appropriate for Valentine's Day, this heart-shaped shell ornament heralds the arrival of spring. (Margaret Furlong Designs, Salem, Ore.)

Right: Don't limit the variety of items you combine! The romantic elegance of Fenton art glass, mixed with these lovable characters created by Karen Germany, form a harmonious and playful pageant atop this oak sideboard.

Above: This collector has certainly hit a high note with a charming arrangement of Easter fare. Busy bunnies frolic atop the piano, serenading the start of spring and beckoning young hands to come explore. Heirloom linens placed beneath would soften the display and create a bit of a contrast between the pieces.

Left: Design a frightful, yet delightful Halloween hamlet on your mantle or bookcase. These little tricksters, part of the Ladie and Friends family, are sure to scare up a treat as the little darlings vie for your affection. Ghost and goblins adorn this ornamental tree from Flambro.

Creative Collector

Personalize an ornament and use it in place of a cake decoration or gift card.

The possibilities for decorating with ornaments are endless—and the opportunities abound year round!

Heat up summer with a hot decorating idea! Armed with Old Glory, a precious parade of patriots celebrates Independence Day atop this coffee table. A lifelike Sandicast critter watches over them.

The possibilities for decorating with ornaments are endless—and the opportunities abound year round! Appropriately in character with Christmas, this arresting wreath, an elegant twist on the traditional nativity, relates a warm welcome to guests. Boughs of fresh-cut greenery are graced with a simple reminder of the true meaning of the holiday. Too pretty for the front door? Hang it above your traditional nativity scene or in a front window—decorative side facing out—for all to see. (Hallmark Cards, Kansas City, Mo.)

It's fun to rotate your collection with the holidays. Posted just inside the entry, these ghastly ghouls greet trick-or-treaters with a bit of All Hallows humor.

Village pieces continue to rise in popularity, perhaps because they allow collectors a passport to "pretend land." The small-scale structures lend themselves to an endless array of decorating options. Branches and boughs, carefully woven to create an attractive border, help hide electrical cords and add an intriguing texture to the snowy winter scene, which can be displayed until spring. Twig trees bare of leaves create an outdoorsy feel. (Department 56, Eden Prairie, Minn.)

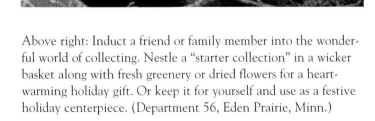

Creative Collector You can easily get your money's worth out of ornaments by displaying them year round. Look for themes that lend themselves to different seasons and incorporate them in a variety of settings from the bath to the bedroom.

Above right: Induct a friend or family member into the wonderful world of collecting. Nestle a "starter collection" in a wicker basket along with fresh greenery or dried flowers for a heartwarming holiday gift. Or keep it for yourself and use as a festive holiday centerpiece. (Department 56, Eden Prairie, Minn.)

Right: Set atop a piano, the splendor of this scurrying cityscape creates a cozy spot for singing holiday hymns. Pine sprigs festooned with festive ribbon complete the look of this wintry wonderland. (Department 56, Eden Prairie, Minn.)

Creative Collector

Remember that Christmas is a holiday for kids of all ages. By incorporating items they will enjoy, you will create a more festive atmosphere. Not thrilled about having Ren and Stimpy, Superman, or Ronald McDonald on your elegantly attired tree? Let your kids have their own miniature in their room. My eleven-year-old son has his own collection of colored lights, tinsel, and ornaments. He has a blast each year unpacking things he hasn't seen since last Christmas and he looks forward to purchasing new pieces each year! Santa usually leaves at least one in his stocking.

Collectibles speak volumes without saying a word. Here the triumphs of traditions long lived are put on display for all to recall. The charming scene, sculpted in simple white porcelain, reminds us of the magic of Christmas. (Department 56, Eden Prairie, Minn.)

A fire may warm the home, but Christmas traditions are sure to warm your heart.

Above: It doesn't take a lot of fuss to fabricate a fabulous display featuring your favorite pieces. This lone cottage, simply surrounded with a few accessories, serves as a night-light for the homeowners and adds a whimsical touch to an otherwise plain end table. (Department 56, Eden Prairie, Minn.)

Right: Amusing architectural miniatures provide a pretty-as-a-picture focal point in this Coca-Cola-themed wreath, which acts as a natural frame for the festive vignette. Dried details and a bright bow accentuate the artful arrangement. (The Cavanagh Group International, Roswell, Ga.)

Left: Impish elves and playful polar bear add a little Christmas magic to this evergreen wreath. Artfully accentuated with baby's breath and boldly colored berries that can be replaced after their color begins to fade, an amusing array of character ornaments enlivens the arrangement. (The Cavanagh Group International, Roswell, Ga.)

Below: Tiny miniatures are tucked into the boughs of this smart-looking wreath. Gold spray paint graces sprigs of dried flora that were picked from nearby bushes and are evenly placed throughout. Bright ribbon or a bold bow would add extra appeal. (The Cavanagh Group International, Roswell, Ga.)

Creative Collector Let the glamour of the holidays inspire you. To achieve the look, cover floral foam with sphagnum moss to create a base. Insert ornaments into the foam with floral wire. Fill in bare spots with silk flowers, branches, and greenery.

Covered in colorful boxwood with ornaments capturing a nostalgic St. Nick, this spiraling grapevine takes on the essence of vintage Victoria. The images gracing the ornaments are famous illustrations of the "merry old elf" brought to life by artist Haddon Sundblom. To re-create the look, cover spiral with the greenery of your choice. Attach each ornament with an ornament hook, florist's wire, or vintage ribbon. Add a sparkling strand of white lights for even more holiday magic. (The Cavanagh Group International, Roswell, Ga.)

> Things that catch viewers off guard have the most impact.

Creative Collector

Mounds of woodshaved grass placed under or around spring Easter collectibles create a sense of place and time. Use accessories as you would in a winter village display. Create flower gardens with silk or dried florals.

Creative Collector An Easter wreath welcomes spring with a delightful display of color. Place a large resin bunny or lighted porcelain house, such as the ones by Midwest of Cannon Falls, in the center of a grapevine wreath that has been covered with Spanish moss. Depending on the size and weight, secure the piece with floral wire or hot glue. Alternate silk tulips, daisies, or crocus with dried bulb leaves, which you can dry yourself or purchase at a craft center or floral supply store.

The tone for a lighthearted holiday is already set! Filled with a nostalgic array of cola collectibles, this cozy lodge has been transformed into a winter wonderland. Gracing tree branches and gift bows, the spirited charm of these cherished treasures provides a childlike atmosphere kids of any age would eagerly embrace. (The Cavanagh Group International, Roswell, Ga.)

A pack of cola polar bear are thoughtfully tucked into a cozy vintage trunk. By grouping like items in various shapes and sizes, your arrangements enjoy maximum impact. (The Cavanagh Group International, Roswell, Ga.)

A trio of nesting tables are fanned to offer prominent placement to this miscellany of motion musicals. Boughs of fresh greenery, gently draped, pull the look together. (The Cavanagh Group International, Roswell, Ga.)

Creative Collector

Rotate collections according to season, holiday, or theme to provide a fresh look in your home. Changing them on a regular basis will minimize clutter (perhaps you don't have room to display them all at once) and you will feel like your home is getting a makeover every few weeks. Pack out-of-season items in their original packing and store like themes together for easy retrieval next year.

Santas in every shape and size, depicting countries all over the world, are a passion for this homeowner. Her collection, though on exhibit year round, takes center stage come Christmas. A garland bearing a bounty of blown glass baubles, also in the image of St. Nick, frames the scene nicely.

In celebration of Christmas, elegant embellishments reminiscent of Victorian times emanate a note of holiday cheer. Seraphim take center stage among tiny nosegays and satiny strands of ribbon. Decidedly feminine touches, such as the porcelain prima donnas perched atop the end table, impart an air of romance.

Left: Architectural miniatures depicting various places of worship have become a collecting category all their own. This lighted display featuring churches, cathedrals, and chapels from around the world reminds us of the real reason for the season. Electrical cords are kept under cover using cotton batting that imitates the look of snow.

Using ordinary household items, this collector has created a Lilliputian Bethlehem that incorporates her vast collection of Fontanini figures. Buildings are made from packing boxes, while silk ferns attached to twigs serves as palm trees. Sphagnum and Spanish mosses are intermixed and layered atop stairsteps of plastic foam and sheet moss to create a lifelike landscape. Native limestone, lichen, and pebbles add to the natural effect. (Roman, Inc., Roselle, Ill.)

Creative Collector Present grandma and grandpa with a gift they will treasure for years to come. Create personalized ornaments inscribed with all the grandchildren's names and their dates of birth. Place them on a wreath or wall hanging along with birth announcements, baby photos, and other personal mementos.

Left: Situated in any room, miniature trees are a great way to celebrate a variety of seasonal themes. Here, this cozy breakfast nook gets a cupful of celestial cheer. The items on the plate rail—currently a heralding of angels—can be changed seasonally, although angels are a prominent and popular collectible year round. Notice the homeowner has incorporated figurines and woodcarvings into the plate rail, adding dimension to the display.

Below: Grab your glue gun and make a little magic. You can easily add interest to a plain garden pot by attaching a pretty ornament. Use tiny miniatures featuring birds or flowers to mimic the "garden" theme, or for gift giving, personalize the ornament with the recipient's name. (Hallmark Cards, Kansas City, Mo.)

Creative Collector

Not every ornament comes packaged with a stand, but they are easily purchased through gift and collectibles retailers. Favorites among many collectors are those crafted with a wooden base and an arched hook for hanging. Group several ornaments in simple shapes upon one hook for an intriguing effect. Or cluster three or more hangers, each supporting a single ornament, and vary their heights.

Above: A fire may warm the home, but Christmas traditions are sure to warm your heart. Floral patterns abound in this classic parlor—the room that defined Victorian culture and set the tone for entertaining. From the presentation upon the mantle to the elegantly attired tree, all the best is on display. Group pieces from the same period when displaying your collection in order to carry out the theme.

Right and far right: Use a special ornament in addition to a bow to add some pizzazz to your gift wrap. Coordinate the ornament with your wrapping paper or choose a special something certain to please the lucky recipient. (Hallmark Cards, Kansas City, Mo.)

Add some pizzazz
to your gift wrap.

Imagine cozy gatherings in this reading room. An eight-foot tree (laden with enough ornaments to fill Santa's sleigh) is certain to dazzle adults and delight wee ones. Brimming with blown glass baubles, the swag suitably encircles a print of old St. Nick. Candlesticks are trimmed with tree toppers in place of candles, while gilded garland and stockings stuffed to the brim provide a beguiling hearth. (Christopher Radko Designs, Dobbs Ferry, N.Y.)

Jazz up your old stockings with new ornaments. Sew them on with embroidery thread or bright ribbon. Create personalized ornaments to identify each person's stocking—even grandparents and aunts and uncles can join in the fun with ornaments embossed with their family "title." Or choose a different theme for each family member. Ornaments depicting baseball, football, or soccer would be fitting for the family athlete. Start out a newborn with a stocking embellished with an array of dated "Baby's First Christmas" ornaments. (Hallmark Cards, Kansas City, Mo.)

Because their presentation is so unique, gift baskets have become one of today's most popular gift-giving trends. Fill the basket, or any container appropriate for the recipient or the theme you wish to focus on, with special goodies destined to delight. Top it off with an appropriate ornament that is certain to serve as a treasured keepsake. Personalize a gift basket with a "First Home" ornament for a festive housewarming present, or embellish an Easter basket with a bunny, chick, or colored eggs. (Hallmark Cards, Kansas City, Mo.)

Above: A completed collection of dated annuals calls for a lively display of their unique charm. Each rocking horse can be invisibly attached using floral wire or hot glue. (Hallmark Cards, Kansas City, Mo.)

Above right: Understated yet elegant, this tree demonstrates that a little magic can go a long way. Simple white lights, used sparingly, illuminate bisque shells and gilded goodies. For the most effective lighting, wrap tiny lights close to the tree's trunk. Wind cords around each branch, wrapping the boughs lengthwise to create a more natural lighting pattern. (Margaret Furlong Designs, Salem, Ore.)

Right: Evergreen and ivy enhanced by the solitary placement of a single seraphim grace the top of this gilded frame. The theme is continued upon the elegant tree. (Margaret Furlong Designs, Salem, Ore.)

Far right: The tradition of nutcrackers is as old as they are delightful. This duo offers a nostalgic backdrop and provides a touch of holiday humor. (Midwest of Cannon Falls, Cannon Falls, Minn.)

Nutcrackers provide a touch of holiday humor.

Left: Holiday magic abounds and the signs of the season are everywhere. Don't be afraid to move things around—shake them up a bit. This homeowner has boldly replaced the usual wall hangings with portraits of old St. Nick. She has lavished a little tender loving care on her hutch by generously draping it in evergreen and holly. A sparkling selection of Christopher Radko ornaments adds the crowning glory. (Christopher Radko Designs, Dobbs Ferry, N.Y.)

Decorating for the holidays helps create a more festive atmosphere in which to celebrate. Using lighted village pieces and kooky characters, the children have created their own spooky scene especially for Halloween. By allowing your children to help out, they're certain to be awed by the magic and will grow to appreciate the customs and traditions you have set forth. (Midwest of Cannon Falls, Cannon Falls, Minn.)

Left: Light up your home for Easter with a spring-time village. The cheery palette is a welcome change from winter. Incorporate silk plants or flowers, which serve nicely as landscaping elements and add a realistic touch. (Midwest of Cannon Falls, Cannon Falls, Minn.)

Right: A plate rail offers an easy way to rotate your collection. Switch out pieces to depict different decorating themes, seasons, or holidays. Here, the art of Sandra Kuck becomes the focal point upon this mantle. Add depth to the display by stringing garland along the rail or hanging greenery or a wreath nearby. Because the Thomas Kinkade plates (left) are framed, the scene incorporates a variety of sizes. Notice how the framed pieces have added impact. (The Bradford Exchange, Niles, Ill.)

Perfectly suited for a centerpiece, these villages take on a luminous glow when surrounded by a cavalcade of candles. The insides of each piece are lit with tiny tealights. A wreath of greenery encircles the diminutive vignette. (Department 56, Eden Prairie, Minn.)

Southwest Style

*P*roper" decorating is a thing of the past. No more formal sitting rooms, untouchable furnishings, or hands-off artwork. Today's trend calls for casual, even eclectic, surroundings meant to bring comfort and enjoyment to everyday life.

A love of the American West has lured many a homeowner to display the natural elements of Western style. From Native American art to cowboy kitsch, the best of the West is riding high.

For the serious collector, pewter sculptures, mixed media, and metal art re-create the presence of important historical icons and capture the rugged spirit of the Old West. Comical cowpokes and rustic wranglers portrayed in tiny miniatures (ornaments, teapots, and wood resin figurines) provide a touch of whimsy. These collectibles allude to the relaxed feel enjoyed by those choosing life in this part of the country, or those just seeking some of its spicy flavor. So, saddle up and prepare for a stable of decorating possibilities.

From Native American art to cowboy kitsch, the best of the West is riding high.

Left: Just as the storytellers of Native American cultures wove their fanciful fables, this homeowner has captured the relaxed feel and richly hued palette of the Southwest. By loosely incorporating a variety of pieces such as bronze sculptures, wildlife prints, and Native American figures, she has created an atmosphere indicative of wide-open spaces. Handwoven baskets, rugs, and authentic artifacts add a true touch of the Southwest.

Above right: The cool metal in these mixed media sculptures is contrasted with the warm, earthy tones of an antique rug. Willy Whitten and C. A. Pardell—two of the industry's finest designers of quality pewter pieces—are the artists. Items are arranged so that nothing is the same height or "weight." Heavier pieces take center stage while smaller items fill in, adding balance and texture.

Creative Collector

Frame a Western print with a lasso or lariat. Have your framer incorporate the rope into the actual mat or frame, or arrange a piece in a proportionate circumference so it encircles the framed work.

A lodgepole pine kiva ladder acts efficiently as an easel for this uniquely matted Native American print by Maija. The vibrant turquoise interior of the hutch makes an arresting backdrop for a collection of Ted DeGrazia plates and figurines. The grape-vine sunflower garland, tacked on with tiny nails, frames the display picture perfectly.

Left: This timeworn trastero holds a varied selection of Native American and Hispanic trinkets. An effective use of space is made by placing pieces from the "Sun Village," created by Gregory Perillo, at various heights and depths. A boldly patterned serape adds a spicy touch of Southwest color.

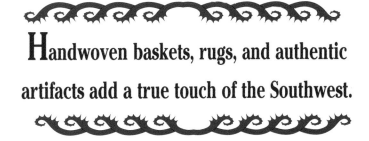

Handwoven baskets, rugs, and authentic artifacts add a true touch of the Southwest.

Creative Collector
Drape a saucy serape across your display surface for a colorful backdrop to your Native American collectibles.

Nutcrackers are available in nearly any image—this grouping of chieftain characters is just a sampling. Complete with colorful headdress and an assortment of handheld accessories, these amusing natives add a spicy-hot flavor to an island table. Display them year round for a funky flair anywhere.

Right: This ample abode features loads of room, and lots of built-in nooks and crannies perfect for displaying Native American art and collectibles. The homeowners were instrumental in the home's design. He crafted much of the furniture with his own hands. She used her interior design instincts to create a livable home filled with diverse items they've gathered for years and will enjoy for many years to come. The amusing elements, such as the Western-attired characters atop the coffee table, have the most impact.

Above: Create a festive setting with an eclectic array of cowboy kitsch. Department 56 ornaments and accessories provide the color; you create the magic.

Right: Red-hot chilies light up this grapevine wreath. The look is completed with a creative use of rope garland and a collection of Department 56 ornaments.

Creative Collector Alternate authentic baskets or weavings with Native American-themed plates or prints.

Right: The surprising elements are always the most enjoyable. Here a kitschy collection of Western-themed teapots elicits lighthearted laughter from visitors. Skinny cowpoke characters—actually ornaments from Department 56—hang from pegs, an amusing addition to this simple shelf.

Left: The colorful art of Ted DeGrazia takes center stage atop this one-of-a-kind cabinet, hand-crafted by the homeowner. Brightly hued horizontal prints make an effective use of wall space.

Below: This bedroom is a young buckaroo's dream. Funky Western relics such as mom's old boots and books combine with fun-loving collectibles to complete the laid-back look of a little cowboy's playful retreat.

Offering hours of amusement, these rockin' rustlers mimic antique versions that have become too expensive for the average collector to procure.

Campy characters and outrageous elements unite to create an offbeat look in this little rustler's bedroom, providing "all a cowboy needs for a good night's sleep."

A cavalcade of cowpokes and a wagon train of cheese rustlers create a fun and funky look. The covered wagon is actually a motion musical from Enesco and serves double as a music maker.

Minute bronzes mixed with a colorful collection of antique kachina dolls and Native American regalia grace the home of these avid collectors of Indian artifacts. The mix of things "old" lends an air of authenticity, while current collectibles, such as mixed media sculptures by Legends, spark interest in new procurements.

Above: Preserving history is something that often triggers the urge to collect. This grouping serves as a pledge to recapture the colorful past of the cowboy—an increasingly popular theme among collectors who long for a link to the past.

Above right: Rustic bronzes re-creating the powerful artistry of Frederic Remington—an artist whose work has enjoyed continued popularity nearly one hundred years after its inception—are situated throughout the room. The format allows each piece to stand on its own merit. (Enesco Corp., Itasca, Ill.)

Right: This homeowner erected a broomstick tree as an inviting addition to the entry. A campy ensemble of ornaments—boots, broncs, hats, and horses—grace the branches, which are bound with white lights and lariat. Sunflowers, her home state's native flower, are wired to the boughs, adding a bright bit of color.

Far right: Native American tapestries serve as a delightful backdrop for this patriotic tree. Situated in the entry, the setup serves as a delightful greeting for visitors. Ocean-themed ornaments provide the "stars" for a stars and stripes tribute. (Margaret Furlong Designs, Salem, Ore.)

A boldly patterned serape adds a spicy touch of color.

Above: Verdigris vessels are combined with a patinated pewter sculpture and wildlife plate in this thoroughly modern home. Though the surroundings are completely contrary to the collectibles, the look is a harmonious blend of styles.

Upper right: Artificial cactus leaves, available at a craft or floral supply store, provide the perfect base for this unique wreath. Santa and Mrs. Claus ornaments from Hallmark add a touch of holiday humor while wishing Feliz Navidad (the Spanish equivalent of Merry Christmas) to collectors. The introduction of items depicting various cultures is an important trend for the industry. (Hallmark Cards, Kansas City, Mo.)

Right: The rustic feel of the Wild West is contrasted against a contemporary backdrop.

This stately Native American sculpture stands alone, speaking volumes without saying a word. Created in mixed media, the statuesque bronze serves as a ruggedly elegant accompaniment to this Southwestern style home. (Lance Corp., Hudson, Mass.)

Victorian Romance

*T*he opulence of the Victorian era has seduced architects, designers, and interior decorators for over a century. Intricate patterns paired with vintage furnishings create elegant surroundings certain to instill an appreciation for the period.

The cavalcade of collectibles inspired by the era includes charming prints of children (Sandra Kuck is an artist who comes to mind), sculptures that offer sweet serenades to lovers, and figurines featuring masses of richly colored roses and vining ivies. Dolls lavished in lace are indicative of the elaborate dresses and gowns worn back then and add a ceremonious note.

Through our search of collectibles inspired by the era, we gathered dozens of ideas. The result is a real page-turner in which romance emanates from collections accumulated with love.

Unusual accompaniments add interest to any collection.

Left: This small but sunny space harbors a collection of angels. Presiding over a posh powder room, their ornate beauty is left to speak for itself. Notice that plates—highly detailed in their artistry—are clustered in small groupings so as not to overpower one another. (The Bradford Exchange, Niles, Ill.)

Right: Take cues from your collection! This hand-painted secretary desk echoes the hand-painted designs indicative of Fenton art glass. Fluted perfume bottles and fancy jewelry boxes surrounded by vintage Victorian valentines add a timeless touch of romance.

Left and below: A bevy of beauties adorns this hutch. The key ingredients in the appealing exhibit are "like" themes and colors in a variety of sizes and mediums grouped to form an arrangement pleasing to the eye.

Right: This nearly forgotten alcove becomes a magical place when cherished collectibles are introduced. Items tossed aside for years suddenly find use. A timeworn church pew, lovingly lined with little ladies, is first draped in a lacy tablecloth. Riding in high style, dolls are grouped in an antique baby buggy—another find from the attic. An elegant lamp provides light and keeps the corner from becoming too dark.

Left: Porcelain dolls (fired, painted, and dressed by the home-owner) are carefully clustered with an arresting array of tots created by artists such as Corrine Layton, Lee Middleton, and Yolanda Bello. Lladró bunnies situated in an antique wall cabinet overlook the pretend tea party.

Above: Items held dear are artfully arranged in this sunny window seat. By incorporating old toys, games, and teddies, new collectibles take on a nostalgic air.

Right: The art of Thomas Kinkade is tastefully arranged in this entry. A colorful canvas, provided by the painted wall, serves as an arresting backdrop. The frames set off the plates' designs and make for a bold contrast. A simple bouquet introduces texture and serves as a nice complement. (The Bradford Exchange, Niles, Ill.)

Left: A parade of M. I. Hummel figurines—testament to the innocence of children—makes its way across this oak dressing table.

Below: Unusual accompaniments add interest to any collection. Here, the homeowner placed an antique time-piece, an heirloom passed down from her grandparents, alongside her collectibles.

Above: Much-loved trinkets and treasures add a touch of nostalgia to this cozy attic arbor. The heartwarming display provides a quiet place for reflecting upon happy memories.

Left: Lacy little darlings and the luminous glow of world-famous Lladró sculptures combine to create a room of timeless appeal.

Left: The elegant allure of a mother's dressing table bespeaks a mystery intriguing girls of all ages. A dab of her perfume, a touch of her makeup, and wee ones feel all grown up. The nostalgic display of enchanting mementos featuring children entices little hands to explore.

Right: Sleeping in an antique bed is like slipping into someone else's dreams. This elegant bridal boudoir, decorated with sentimental wedding mementos, captures the romance of young love and pays tribute to everlasting happiness. The hand-crafted eggs are becoming an increasingly popular medium.

Below: Lavished with lace and tiny treasures, this antique organ holds a cheerful cache of cherished mementos. Fenton art glass and figurines inspired by the artwork of illustrator Maud Humphrey Bogart are the key ingredients. Combined with lacy doilies and dried flowers, these items evoke a strong sense of nostalgia.

Warm up a tight corner by displaying an element of surprise!

Left: This arresting arrangement of porcelain figurines pays tribute to the art of Sister Maria Innocentia Hummel and epitomizes the charm of children. Personal mementos add an intimate touch.

Below: One glance at this fanciful lair and you can almost hear the giddy chatter of young girls eager to play dress-up and explore the land of make-believe.

Creative Collector Take cues from your collection and tint your walls in a shade that plays up their artistry. A bright wall provides a vibrant backdrop for a collage of floral plates, while soft colors cast a glow upon porcelain dolls in vintage lace.

Sleeping in an antique bed is like slipping into someone else's dreams.

Above: Lighted architectural miniatures add a welcoming touch to this entry. Remember, you don't have to amass several pieces to create the feel of a collection. One or two, prominently placed, can be very effective. (Forma Vitrum, Cornelius, N.C.)

Right: Warm up a tight corner by displaying an element of surprise! This stained-glass lighthouse shines bright at night, offering sleepwalkers a steadfast landmark, just as the real thing supplies solace to seamen. (Forma Vitrum, Cornelius, N.C.)

Filled with period furnishings and tag sale treasures, this surprisingly inviting attic offers a quiet respite in which to enjoy the art of Jan Hagara. As one of the industry's most prominent artists, Jan's art can be enjoyed in a variety of mediums. Her portraits of young girls, which are featured on plates, prints, dolls, and figurines, harken back to simpler times and offer a refreshing style that combines elegance and simplicity. (Jan Hagara Collectables, Georgetown, Texas)

Creative Collector

A vertical treatment of miniature plates takes on a new look with a backdrop of wide ribbon or tapestry. Cut a piece of ribbon or fabric about thirty-six to forty-two inches long. The width will depend on the diameter of your plates, but four inches is a good gauge. Make sure to choose a color or pattern that complements your collectibles. Adhere the ribbon to the wall with double-sided tape or tack it on with flat push pins. Spacing them at equal intervals, arrange three plates atop the ribbon by gluing the backsides to the fabric, or by using your usual plate-hanging method. Use the same treatment with miniature prints.

Forget all the mess of electrical cords; illuminate architectural miniatures with tiny tealight candles. They burn for hours and are inexpensively purchased at gift, discount, or grocery stores. (Forma Vitrum, Cornelius, N.C.)

Left: Tiny trees are all it takes to create a vignette atop this end table. To easily accomplish the look of snow—and protect the surface of your fine furnishings— place a piece of cotton batting beneath the setup. (Forma Vitrum, Cornelius, N.C.)

A tiny township transforms this elegant console. The lighted stained glass houses, surrounded by all the usual amenities, create a lively conversation piece. Electrical cords are carefully camouflaged by the potted plant below. (Forma Vitrum, Cornelius, N.C.)

A tiny tabletop holds treasures dear to the heart while creating ambiance in this elegant alcove bath. Resting at tub's edge, plates mimic the floral pattern in the wallpaper and complement the cottage theme in the coordinating plates by artist Marty Bell.

Above: Transform an empty vertical space into a showcase for your collection. The symmetrical alignment of these plates makes the most of wall space and draws the eye upward, making the room appear larger. Topiaries frame the display, adding texture and interest. (The Bradford Exchange, Niles, Ill.)

Right: Pieces from Department 56's "New England Village" provide a festive focal point for this feast. Light up miniature abodes with tiny candles placed inside. Tuck greenery or grape-vine into the scene to create an outdoor feel. For an elegant glow, arrange simple votives around the perimeter. (Department 56, Eden Prairie, Minn.)

Forget all the mess of electrical cords; illuminate architectural miniatures with tiny tealight candles.

Does the living room seem an unlikely repository for a collection of dolls? Prized possessions should appear anywhere you want to add a touch of personality! The key is not to "over amass" them all in one place. Spread them out and integrate plates, prints, and figurines in like themes or genres. Tuck in vintage photos or keepsakes important only to you. These newly designed spaces will provide you much pleasure day after day.

Romance is in the air year round when you exhibit a love affair with collectibles. Here the flight of fancy created by Fenton art glass and Swarovski silver crystal deliver a heart-piercing arrow from cupid. The sleek design of a single Lladró silently bespeaks volumes of poetic prose.

Don't reserve dolls for the bedroom. This sophisticated sweetheart stands sentry in the entry, welcoming guests and enticing them to explore your home.

Left: For lovers only, this romantic Lladró bride and groom figurine would make a delightful presentation to your favorite newlyweds. The item is certain to become a treasured heirloom and may even start the couple on their way to collecting. The gift could be given ahead of time for use as a cake topper on the big day. (Lladró USA, Moonachie, N.J.)

Right: This corner takes on a new shape with the bewitching influence of figures decidedly feminine. The work of Steve Hanks, an artist known for his ability to faithfully capture the sensual beauty of women, is thoughtfully displayed alongside an innocent and intriguing doll.

Transform an empty vertical space into a showcase for your collection.

Left: The breathtaking grace of Lladró is unique unto itself. Flowing fabrics cling seductively as sweet faces shine bright. This figurine provides an alluring appointment upon this hall table. (Lladró USA, Moonachie, N.J.)

Right: A cascade of foliage falls gracefully from this grapevine wreath, alluding to the elegant figures featured below. The unique painting treatment of the wall was laboriously achieved by the homeowner, and creates a colorful backdrop for collectibles.

Richly appointed surroundings call for equally elegant collectibles. Perhaps nothing compares to the sleek lines and soft hues of the art of Lladró. These figures, placed where the collector spends time deep in thought, are obviously highly prized. (Lladró USA, Moonachie, N.J.)